DATE DUE

POINT OF IMPACT

Revised and Updated

Heinemann Library
Chicago, Illinois

Hiroshima

The Shadow of the Bomb

© 2000, 2006 Heinemann Library
a division of Reed Elsevier Inc.
Chicago, Illinois

Customer Service 888-454-2279
Visit our website at www.heinemannraintree.com

Designed by Tokay Interactive Ltd. (www.tokay.co.uk)
Printed in China by WKT Ltd

10 09 08 07 06
10 9 8 7 6 5 4 3 2 1

New edition ISBNs:1-40349-140-2 (hardcover)
              1-40349-149-6 (paperback)

The Library of Congress has cataloged the first edition as follows:
Tames, Richard.
        Hiroshima : the shadow of the bomb / Richard Tames.
            p. cm. -- (Point of Impact)
        Includes bibliographical references and index.
        ISBN 1-57572-414-6
        1. Hiroshima-shl (Japan)--History--Bombardment, 1945--Juvenile literature. 2. World
War, 1939-1945--Japan--Hiroshima-shi--Juvenile literature. 3. Atomic bomb--Juvenile
literature. [1. Hiroshima-shi (Japan)--History--Bombardment, 1945. 2. World War,
1939-1945--Japan--Hiroshima-shi. 3. Atomic bomb.] I. Title. II. Series.

        D767.25.H6 T34 2000
        940. 54'25--dc21
                                                        00-(24346

Acknowledgments
The publishers would like to thank the following for permission to reproduce photographs:
Corbis-Bettmann/UPI, pp.**4**, **14**, **15**, **16**, **25**, **27**; Corbis/Reuters/Christian Charisius. p. **29**;
Honeywell, Chris, p.**7**; Popperfoto, pp.**6**, **12**, **18**, **22**, **23**, **26**; Tames, Richard, pp.**8**, **20**, **21**;
TRH Pictures, pp.**11**, **19**.

Cover photograph reproduced with permission of Getty Images / Time Life Pictures / Pix Inc. /
Alfred Eisenstadt.

The publishers would like to thank Stewart Ross for his help in the preparation of this book.

Contents

Some words are shown in bold, **like this**. You can find out what they mean by looking in the Glossary.

What Happened at Hiroshima?

An unsuspecting city

On August 6, 1945, the Japanese city of Hiroshima awoke to a beautiful, sunny morning. Although World War II (1939–45) had ended in Europe, Japan was fighting on, and it was being bombed heavily. As the citizens of Hiroshima went about their daily business, they were unaware that the lives of thousands of them would shortly come to a terrifying, violent end. The United States had selected their city as the target for the world's first atomic bomb attack.

Just before 9 A.M., a U.S. B29 bomber, the *Enola Gay*, appeared over Hiroshima. It was carrying a single atomic bomb weighing 9,900 pounds (4,500 kilograms). Although many tests had been done, nobody knew for certain what the effect of dropping an atomic bomb on a major city would be.

Death from the sky

The co-pilot, Colonel Paul Tibbets, released the bomb, and the *Enola Gay* quickly climbed to safety. Less than a minute later, the bomb exploded. One eyewitness saw a flash so bright she thought a fire had started in her eyes.

A shadow over the world: the Hiroshima bomb created this mushroom cloud.

She then realized that the skin on her face, hands, and arms had peeled off. Although they could not see the devastation through the huge cloud of smoke and dust, one of the *Enola Gay*'s crew cried out, "My God, what have we done?" The explosion produced a ground temperature of 5,400 °F (3,000 °C)—twice as high as the melting point of iron. An estimated 50,000 people living within 0.6 miles (1 kilometer) of the blast burned to death. A wind tore through the city at 500 miles (800 kilometers) per hour, uprooting trees and flattening buildings.

Survivors staggered around in a state of shock. The dead and dying lay all around. People tried to help each other, but there was chaos everywhere. This city of 245,000 people only had 150 doctors. Of these, 65 were killed and most of the rest were wounded. Of 1,780 nurses, 1,654 were dead or too injured to work. At the city's biggest hospital, only 1 doctor out of 30 was uninjured and only 5 more were able to work. The nursing staff of over 200 was down to 10. Ten thousand wounded poured in desperately seeking help.

Hiroshima was a medium-sized port and industrial center backed by a ring of mountains that enclosed the force of the blast.

The final toll

No one knows exactly how many died in Hiroshima on August 6, 1945. Official figures estimated 100,000. As the months went by, the figure rose steadily. **Radiation** sickness was taking its toll. By the end of 1945, the estimate was 140,000.

Death march

On August 7, 1945, the day after the bomb was dropped, a Japanese doctor wrote in his diary:

"Hundreds of injured people trying to escape passed our house. Their hands and faces were burned and swollen; great sheets of skin had peeled away like rags on a scarecrow. By this morning there were so many of them lying on both sides of the road it was impossible to pass without stepping on them."

How the Atom Bomb Changed the World

The first successful atom bomb test had taken place in July 1945.
Robert J. Oppenheimer, whose team of scientists made the bomb,
said afterward, "We knew the world would not be the same."
Other people agreed.

On September 2, 1945, less than a month after the atomic bombing of
Japan, Douglas MacArthur, a U.S. general, warned that a nuclear war
could destroy the entire human race. The terrifying power of atomic
weapons made military leaders realize that any country thinking about
using one might easily bring disaster on itself as well as on its enemy.
U.S. General Omar Bradley concluded, "The way to win an atomic war is
to make certain it never starts."

Hiroshima was devastated
by the bomb.

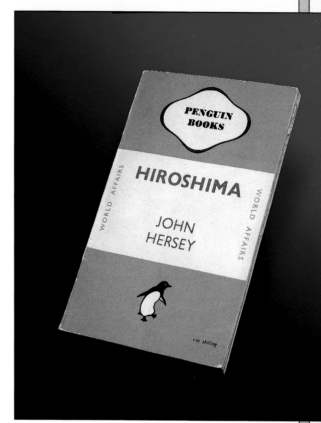

Telling the world

In May 1946, the *New Yorker* magazine sent journalist John Hersey to Japan to find survivors of the attack on Hiroshima. He interviewed two doctors, two priests, and two women and wrote about what they had suffered and seen. The *New Yorker*'s editor was shocked by Hersey's 30,000-word report. He believed that most people still did not understand how terrible the effects of an atom bomb were.

The *New Yorker* published Hersey's complete account in a single issue. The editor thought this would have more impact than spreading it over several weekly issues. He was right. It sold out within hours. Fifty U.S. newspapers reprinted it. It was broadcast on the radio in both the United States and the United Kingdom. In the United States, the Book of the Month Club published it as a special "extra." In the United Kingdom, Penguin Books printed 250,000 paperback copies of it.

The value of fear

In November 1945, Albert Einstein, the world's most famous scientist, wrote:

"I do not believe that civilization will be wiped out in a war fought with the atomic bomb. Perhaps two-thirds of the people of the earth might be killed, but enough men capable of thinking, and enough books, would be left to start again, and civilization could be restored. Since I do not foresee that atomic energy is to be a great **boon** for a long time, I have to say that for the present it is a menace. Perhaps it is as well that it should be. It may **intimidate** the human race into bringing order into its international affairs, which, without the pressure of fear, it would not do."

The Background: How Japan Became a Threat

Opening up the closed country

In 1639, after many years of civil war, Japan cut off trade with other countries, fearing outsiders might cause more problems. In 1853 a modern U.S. fleet demanded the right to trade. Japan had fallen far behind in technology and was forced to agree. This humiliation caused years of crisis and confusion, but by 1873 a new government was in power, determined to make Japan strong by adopting Western-style technology. It used foreign experts and imports to rapidly modernize the armed forces, build railroads, and set up cotton mills and steelworks. Western-style banks, schools, coinage, weights and measures, newspapers, and postal services were introduced.

Empire building

Japan's leaders compared their country to Great Britain, a small offshore island. By conquering a huge overseas empire, Britain had become the most powerful country in the world. Japan wanted to do the same. In 1894 Japan and China fought for control over their neighbor, Korea.

Japan modernized its army.

This map shows the growth of the Japanese overseas empire.

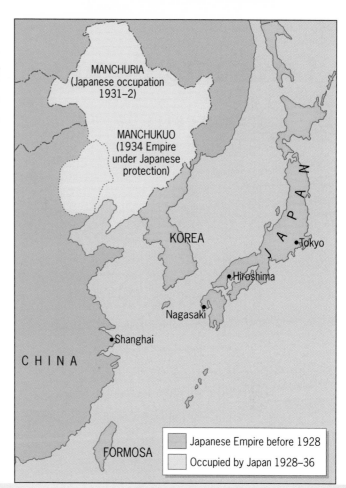

MANCHURIA
(Japanese occupation 1931–2)

MANCHUKUO
(1934 Empire
under Japanese
protection)

KOREA

JAPAN

•Tokyo

•Hiroshima

Nagasaki

•Shanghai

CHINA

FORMOSA

Japanese Empire before 1928

Occupied by Japan 1928–36

Despite its huge population, China was easily defeated by Japan's more modern armed forces. Japan not only took control of Korea, but also took the Chinese island of Taiwan as the first **colony** of its overseas empire. In 1904–45 Japan fought Russia for control of Korea and won. In 1910 Korea became part of the Japanese Empire. These successes gave Japan's military leaders powerful influence within the government.

Tokyo transformed

U.S. teacher W. E .Griffiths was shocked by how poor Japan was when he arrived in rural Echizen in 1870. Within a year, he'd been transferred to the capital, Tokyo, and was amazed by how it had changed in such a short time:

"Tokyo is so modernized that I scarcely recognize it. There are no beggars on the streets. The age of pantaloons [pants] has come. Carriages are numerous. The soldiers are all in uniform, as are the police. New bridges span the canals. Gold and silver coins are being used as money in circulation."

Problems at home

Despite dramatic progress in building modern industries, Japan still had many problems. Rapid population growth kept many people in poverty. In 1923 a massive earthquake destroyed the capital, Tokyo, and the port of Yokohama, killing 100,000 people and destroying or damaging three million homes. The United States gave millions of dollars to help Japan recover, but in 1924 it banned **immigration** by Japanese people. Many Japanese saw this ban as racial prejudice.

Crisis and Conquest

A greater Japan

During the 1920s, **extremists** became more active in politics and in the Japanese army. They argued that the best way for Japan to become rich and respected was to make its empire even bigger. This would provide Japanese industry with the raw materials it needed, such as coal, iron, rubber, and oil, and poor people could leave Japan and start new lives overseas or in the colonies.

Bullying China

Japanese businesses built mines and railroads and mined for minerals in Manchuria, a huge underpopulated part of northern China. The weak Chinese government even allowed Japanese troops to guard the mines and railroads. Between 1929 and 1931, world trade collapsed and millions of people lost their jobs. Three million people were out of work in Japan. The country's leaders desperately wanted to expand. In 1931 the Japanese army faked a Chinese attack on a Manchurian railroad, then used this as an excuse to take over the whole area. In 1937 Japanese generals invaded the rest of China. Three years later, Japan took over French colonies in Southeast Asia.

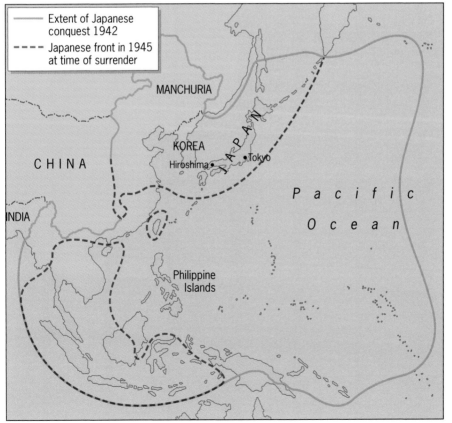

This shows Japanese expansion, 1942–45.

Success in the Pacific

The United States protested against Japan's actions. The U.S. government tried to stop Japan's expansion by refusing to sell its government oil or steel, but Japan still would not withdraw from its conquests. Believing war with the United States was unavoidable, in December 1941 the Japanese air force made a devastating surprise attack on the U.S. naval base at Pearl Harbor, Hawaii. For the next six months, Japanese forces triumphed everywhere. They took the Philippines from the United States and Hong Kong and took Singapore from the United Kingdom.

This shows the attack on Pearl Harbor.

The tide turns

Then, in June 1942, the Japanese lost four aircraft carriers in an important naval battle off Midway Island in the Pacific Ocean. The weakened Japanese navy was now unable to stop U.S. forces from recapturing Pacific islands. By 1944 the United States could send bombers against Japan. Bombing Japan was one thing, but invading Japan was quite another. U.S. forces were about to discover just how fiercely the Japanese would defend their territory.

The price of victory

In April 1945, U.S. forces landed on the offshore Japanese island of Okinawa. It took three months to conquer it. During the fighting, 110,000 of its 120,000 Japanese defenders died. Thirty-four U.S. ships were sunk and 368 damaged, while 12,500 U.S. men were killed and 36,600 wounded. If that was the price to be paid for taking one island of 500 square miles (800 square kilometers), what would it cost to take Japan itself?

Origins of the Atom Bomb

Atoms all around

Everything is made up of atoms, including you. In solid things, the atoms are packed close together. In liquids and gases, they move around more. Atoms are incredibly small—the period at the end of this sentence has 250 billion atoms in it. However, atoms themselves are made up of even smaller particles.

Scientists working in different countries—such as the New Zealander Ernest Rutherford, the Italian-American Enrico Fermi, and the German Albert Einstein—gradually came to understand how atoms are made up. They realized it might be possible to build a device that could make these smaller atomic particles crash into each other in a massive series of mini-collisions, which would release huge amounts of energy.

If these reactions could be controlled, they could produce power for industry—or a devastating new weapon. By the 1930s, scientists in most leading industrial countries were aware that it might be possible to create an "atomic bomb." Whichever country succeeded in doing so first would control a weapon more destructive than any previously invented.

Albert Einstein was the 20th century's most famous scientist.

Letter to the president

On August 2, 1939, just one month before the outbreak of World War II in Europe, Albert Einstein wrote to U.S. President Franklin D. Roosevelt to warn him how recent scientific research could revolutionize warfare:

"Some recent work by E. Fermi and L. [Leo] Szilard leads me to expect that the element uranium may be turned into a new and important source of energy in the immediate future. This would also lead to the construction of bombs. A single bomb of this type, carried by boat and exploded in a port, might very well destroy the whole port, together with some of the surrounding territory. However, such bombs might very well prove too heavy for transportation by air."

A single neutron splits an atom, releasing energy and more neutrons, which creates a chain reaction.

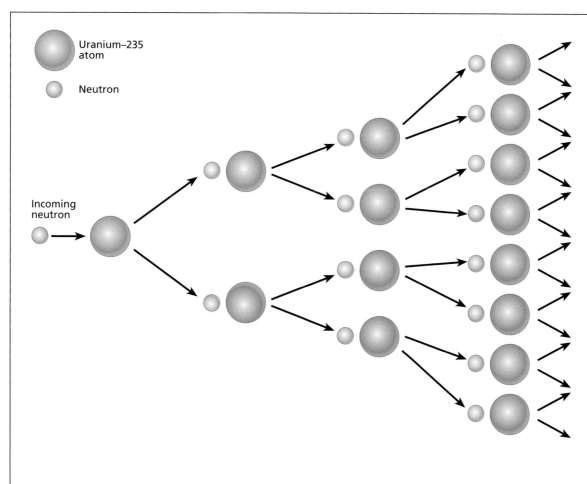

Uranium–235 atom

Neutron

Incoming neutron

The (Almost) Best-Kept Secret of the War

The Manhattan Project

The Manhattan Project was the top-secret effort to build an atomic bomb. It took its code name from the area of New York where the early research was done. The scientists working in the United States included Americans, Britons, Canadians, and European **refugees**. Their work needed large workshops and laboratories and a lot of special technical equipment. Project centers were also built at remote sites in Tennessee, Washington state, and New Mexico. The project cost over $2 billion.

The first test

The first atomic bomb was successfully exploded at Alamagordo air base, in New Mexico, on July 16, 1945. Placed on a steel tower, it created an explosion equal to over 20,000 tons of TNT (an explosive). The heat was so intense that the tower simply disappeared and the desert sand 2,300 feet (700 meters) around its site was turned to glass.

Top secret?

Only the most important **Allied** leaders and generals knew of the atom bomb project.

"Little Boy" was the bomb that wiped out a city.

Not quite

German-born Klaus Fuchs, who worked on the Manhattan Project, was also a **Soviet** agent. His secret reports kept Josef Stalin, the leader of the **USSR**, informed about the bomb project.

The war in Europe had already ended when the first bomb was exploded, but thousands of men were being transported to East Asia to prepare for the invasion of Japan. The war there was expected to last at least another year and a half. Nobody knew that it would be over within a month.

Japanese efforts to make an atomic bomb had been held back by shortages of staff and money. The scientists themselves did not think the matter was urgent, because they believed that even the United States would be able to make one in the foreseeable future. German scientists had also been trying to make an atomic bomb, but gave up when Norwegian resistance fighters **sabotaged** the underground factory that was making the material they needed.

Robert J. Oppenheimer and General Leslie Groves examine the remains of the steel tower that had supported the first successfully exploded A-bomb.

A Japanese bomb?

In 1949 researcher Chitoshi Yanaga admitted that when news about Hiroshima leaked through to them, "Japanese scientists knew immediately that it was the atomic bomb, for they too had been working on it for years." In the two weeks between Japan's surrender and the arrival of U.S. occupation forces, much of the evidence of this work was deliberately destroyed.

No Alternative?

Raids fail to break Japan

In March 1945, 300 U.S. bombers launched a massive night raid on Tokyo. In just two hours, 89,000 people were killed and 130,000 were injured. Many burned alive, others choked for lack of oxygen, and others drowned seeking safety in the Tsumida River. Over the next week, the big industrial cities of Nagoya, Osaka, and Kobe were similarly attacked, but Japan still fought on.

Unconditional surrender

In May 1945, Germany surrendered to the Allies. In July the leaders of the United States, USSR, and the United Kingdom met at Potsdam in Germany to agree to the terms of peace in Europe. They called on Japan to surrender without any conditions, giving up all its overseas conquests. The only promise the Allies made was that the Japanese would not be enslaved nor their country destroyed if they surrendered. Experts on Japan advised the Allied leaders that ordinary Japanese people would obey their government despite hardship, and that an invasion would cost many lives.

At Potsdam, (front row, left to right) Stalin of the USSR, Truman of the U.S., and Clement Attlee of the United Kingdom met.

The decision to drop the atomic bomb

U.S. President Harry S. Truman claimed that he never had any doubts about using the atomic bomb to speed up the end of the war and avoid the need for a bloody invasion.

Some historians have suggested that he also wanted to demonstrate the bomb's immense power to the USSR. The United States and the USSR had never been comfortable as allies because the United States wanted to hold back the spread of **communism**.

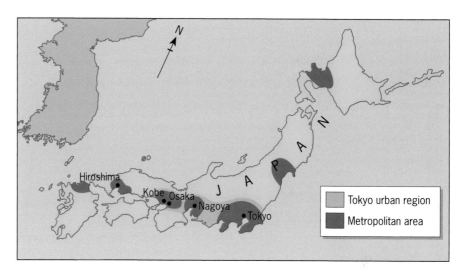

This map shows Japan's big industrial cities in 1945.

Others ask why the Allies did not explode an atomic bomb offshore as a warning. This would have given Japan another chance to surrender before the bomb was actually used on a city. Perhaps the scientists were not 100 percent sure it would really work.

Dropping the bomb

Professor Leo Szilard of the Manhattan Project: "We scientists thought we were in a neck-and-neck race with the Germans and that getting the bomb first might mean the difference between winning and losing the war. But, when Germany was defeated, many of us became uneasy about the proposed use of the bomb in the war with Japan."

U.S. Admiral William Leahy: "The use of this barbarous weapon was of no material assistance. The Japanese were already defeated because of the effective sea **blockade** and successful bombing."

Hisatsune Sakomizu, secretary to the Japanese cabinet: "The atomic bomb (A-bomb) sacrificed many people other than Japanese military. This provided us with an excuse to end the war to save innocent Japanese civilians. If the A-bomb had not been dropped we would have had great difficulty in finding a good reason to end the war."

Why Did Japan Surrender?

Soldiering on

On August 7, 1945, the day after Hiroshima's destruction, Japanese radio simply announced that Japan had been attacked with "a new kind of bomb." No contact was made with the Allies. Instead Japan, which was not at war with the USSR, tried to persuade the Russians to become a go-between to start **negotiations** for peace. On August 8, the Japanese ambassador met the Soviet foreign minister and was told that the USSR was declaring war on Japan. Two hours later, Soviet troops invaded Manchuria.

The second bomb

On August 9, a second A-bomb was dropped on the port of Nagasaki. Although it was much more powerful than the Hiroshima bomb, it did less damage because the city's hilly site lessened the force of the blast. Even so, about 50,000 people died and one-third of all buildings were completely destroyed.

Some Japanese generals still wanted to fight on. Japan is very mountainous—an ideal country for **guerrilla** fighting. Resistance like that seen during the defense of Okinawa could perhaps cost an invader a million casualties. Japanese extremists planned desperate measures, even arming civilians with bamboo spears. They were prepared to fight on, with civilians prepared to suffer high casualties in order to defend Japan and force a negotiated peace.

The Japanese government was completely divided over what to do. In the end, the emperor broke the deadlock, and Japan surrendered on August 14, 1945.

Nagasaki was a major ship-building center.

Were the bombs decisive?

It seemed obvious to many people that the atom bombs hastened the end of the war and so saved the lives an invasion would have cost. However, the war might have been ended in other ways. Ordinary bombing could have continued, without a land invasion, until Japan gave in. Some Japanese leaders feared that their rice fields might be fire-bombed just before harvest. Then, the country would have starved.

Living in the ashes: a Japanese family camps out in the ruins of their Nagasaki home.

Were the USSR's actions decisive?

Some people argue that the USSR's declaration of war against Japan speeded up Japan's surrender. They suggest that the Japanese leaders feared that the USSR and the U.S.-led Allies would invade and permanently divide Japan among them. This is actually what happened to Germany. Another, even worse possibility was that the USSR alone would occupy Japan, get rid of the emperor, and establish communism. Since the Japanese wanted to keep their old ways of ruling, surrendering quickly to the United States, which was likely to be a less brutal occupier, seemed the best option.

Occupation and Reconstruction

A positive partnership

When U.S. troops landed in Japan on August 28, 1945, both sides feared violence. The Americans expected **fanatics** to make sneak attacks on them. The Japanese were afraid their homes would be looted. In fact, the occupation turned out better than anyone had dared hope. The Japanese military disarmed obediently. The Allies decided not to blame the emperor for the war, but rather to use his authority to get Japanese cooperation in carrying out important reforms:

- Japan became a **democracy**. All men and women were given the vote and equal legal rights. Free **trade unions** were allowed.

- Land was given to poor farmers. No one was allowed to own big estates.

- School textbooks that had praised war were rewritten. Education was opened up to more people, especially to women.

The commander of the Allied occupation forces, General Douglas MacArthur, became very popular with the Japanese. The emperor went out in civilian clothes, not military uniform, and met ordinary people face to face for the first time.

Emperor Hirohito dressed in civilian clothes after the war.

Rebuilding from the ashes

The new Japan is peaceful and prosperous.

By the end of the war, Japan had lost 80 percent of its shipping. Bombing had destroyed one-third of all industrial machinery and one-quarter of all buildings. Only the ancient cities of Kyoto, Nara, and Kamakura had been spared. If U.S. forces had not brought in emergency food supplies, many Japanese would have starved in the first winter after the war. In 1955 Japan's living standards were as high as they had been in 1936, and it had manufactured the world's first transistor radio. By 1964 Japan was rich enough to host the Olympics and was making 400 million radios a year.

The benefits of war

U.S. historian John Dower argues that the war boosted Japanese industry:

"In the long view, the Japanese benefited by losing the war. The destruction caused by the air raids actually hastened the construction of more up-to-date factories. Of the 11 major auto manufacturers in post-war Japan, 10 came out of the war years. Shipping, cameras, binoculars, watches, and the like were similarly grounded in technologies given priority during the war. Sewing machines were produced by factories converted from making machine guns. The number of technical schools increased from 11 to over 400 between 1935 and 1945."

A Long Time Dying

Almost everyone within 0.6 miles (1 kilometer) of the center of the atom bomb explosions died—most instantly, the rest within a week—as a result of burns or internal bleeding from organs damaged by the blast. Anyone who was in either city within 100 hours of the explosion received a dangerous dose of radiation.

After-effects of the atom bomb

Many survivors who were not badly burned later developed sores, lost their hair, or suffered from **cataracts** on their eyes. Severe burn victims were disfigured by hard, swollen scars. Radiation victims were prone to blood diseases and cancers. Sixty babies born to mothers exposed to radiation had abnormally small heads; half of these failed to achieve normal levels of intelligence.

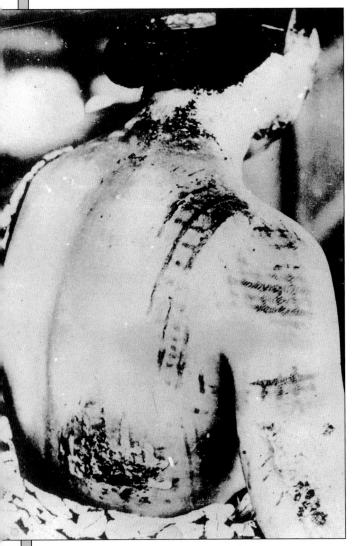

Most atomic bomb survivors, known as *hibakusha* in Japanese, faced a life of poor health and poverty. In 1951 Japan signed a **treaty** with the United States. The Americans would leave Japan, but in return, Japan had to give up any claim against the United States for compensation for the *hibakusha*.

Caring for survivors

Hibakusha formed self-help groups and campaigned for help from the Japanese government. In 1957 the Japanese government finally passed a law giving them free medical care. About 360,000 people qualified for it.

This A-bomb victim has burn scars.

In 1968 the government announced special payments for *hibakusha,* but by 1976 only about one-third of them had received some aid. The city governments of Hiroshima and Nagasaki, supported by charities, took the lead in caring for the *hibakusha* through special hospitals, nursing homes, orphanages, and workshops. Since 1946 both cities have held annual memorial services for victims and have supported organizations working for world peace.

Symbol of survival

The concrete-domed trade center, which survived the Hiroshima explosion, became the center of a peace park. A museum was built there and peace rallies were held. A proposal to demolish the ruined building was angrily rejected by an organization of A-bomb survivors:

"We surviving victims have made a solemn pledge that the same terrible disaster must never be repeated. We should retain the dome as a monument dedicated to peace for all mankind. The atomic bomb is known to all the world, but only for its power. It is still not known what hell the Hiroshima people went through, nor how they continue to suffer from radiation illnesses even today, 19 years after the bombing."

In 1966 the Hiroshima city government voted that the building should be permanently preserved.

The Hiroshima Dome was built as a trade exhibition center. This steel-reinforced concrete structure was directly under the center of the blast.

Cold War and Beyond

Cold War

During World War II, the communist USSR and the Western democracies had joined together to fight Nazi Germany. However, they supported two different ways of living and could not work together after the war. The USSR helped communists take over governments throughout Eastern Europe. This alarmed the West. A "Cold War" rivalry developed, with each side building up weapons and military alliances. In 1949 the democracies formed the North Atlantic Treaty Organization (NATO) under U.S. leadership. That same year the USSR tested its first atomic bomb, showing that both sides now had them. In 1952 the United States tested the world's first H-(hydrogen) bomb, which was far more powerful than the Hiroshima bomb. By 1953 the USSR also had the H-bomb. In 1955 the USSR founded a communist military alliance, called the Warsaw Pact.

Crisis over Cuba

In October 1962, the world came to the edge of war when the USSR sent ships to pro-communist Cuba to install nuclear missiles targeted on the United States. U.S. President John F. Kennedy ordered the U.S. Navy to prevent the Soviet ships from reaching Cuba.

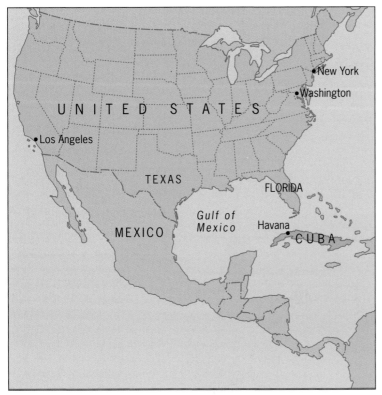

The Cuban Missile Crisis.

To avoid the risk of nuclear war, just in time the Soviet leader Nikita Khrushchev ordered his ships home. Afterward, a "hotline" was set up so that U.S. and Soviet leaders could talk directly in an emergency.

In 1963 the first of a series of agreements was made that limited the testing and spread of nuclear weapons. When the Cold War ended with the collapse of the USSR in 1990, the threat of nuclear conflict was much reduced.

Ongoing danger

Despite international agreements, however, the number of countries with nuclear weapons continued to grow. By 2005 the official list was China, France, India, Israel, Pakistan, Russia, the United Kingdom, and the United States. There were fears that North Korea and Iran were also trying to get hold of them.

People protest for nuclear disarmament.

Ban the bomb!

In Western countries, many people support **disarmament**. In the United States, in 1957 the Committee for a Sane Nuclear Policy (SANE) was formed. The group, supported by high-profile Americans such as Eleanor Roosevelt and Hollywood actors, worked to educate the public about the dangers of nuclear weapons. Their rallies and marches attracted thousands of people. In 1987 the group merged with the Nuclear Weapons Freeze Campaign. Now called Peace Action, the group continues to organize rallies, educate the public, and influence laws made in Washington, D.C.

Atoms for Peace

Pioneering uses

In 1951 the United Kingdom opened the world's first center to treat cancer by using radioactive **cobalt** manufactured in Canada. Over the next 30 years, thirteen million years of human life were saved by this method.

In 1954 the world's first atomic power station, with a capacity of 5,000 **kilowatts**, began generating electricity near Moscow, in the USSR. The first large atomic power station, with a capacity to generate 90,000 kilowatts, opened at Calder Hall in Cumbria, England, in 1956. By 1990 the United States had over 100 nuclear power plants.

The U.S. Navy realized that nuclear power could be used to keep ships sailing for long periods without needing to refuel. In 1954 it launched the world's first atomic-powered submarine, *Nautilus*. Its first voyage lasted

two years and covered over 68,000 miles (110,000 kilometers). In 1958 *Nautilus* made the first-ever journey under the ice cap of the North Pole in just 96 hours.

International cooperation

In 1955 an International Conference on the Peaceful Uses of Atomic Energy was held in Switzerland. Scientists from 73 countries were able to meet together for the first time and learn from each other's work.

USS *Nautilus* was the first atomic-powered submarine.

The head of the fire department that fought the Chernobyl blaze points out the power station's damaged reactor.

Changing views

By the 1980s, people were having serious doubts about nuclear power. Accidents, such as those at Chernobyl (see below), and the problem of disposing of the radioactive waste from nuclear plants made it appear expensive and dangerous. However, by the 21st century, attitudes were changing again. Oil and gas supplies were running low and both these fuels produce serious pollution and contribute to global warming. Looking for a reliable source of environmentally friendly energy, governments around the world were once again considering nuclear power.

Meltdown!

In 1979 a serious accident occurred at the atomic power plant at Three Mile Island, near Harrisburg, Pennsylvania. One hundred thousand residents had to be moved temporarily because of the danger from escaping gases. It was later shown that workers had not understood what was happening and had turned off safety devices by mistake. The worst nuclear accident to date happened at Chenobyl in the Ukraine in 1986. A reactor exploded during an experiment, killing 31 workers and sending 500 more to the hospital. Everyone living within 19 miles (30 kilometers) was evacuated. Winds carried radioactive fallout as far away as Wales, in the United Kingdom. Ten years later, the area around Chernobyl was still poisoned, and local people suffered above-average levels of cancer, leukemia, and other illnesses caused by radiation.

27

The Great Debate

The use of nuclear bombs on Japan in 1945, the spread of nuclear weapons since then, and the peaceful use of nuclear energy are all hotly debated.

Question 1: Was the bombing of Japan right?

Yes!

- It helped the war to end quicker than would have happened otherwise.
- In the long run, it saved lives.
- It frightened off the USSR from trying to spread communism by force.

No!

- The bombs were dropped without warning—the threat of using them should have been tried first.
- Thousands of innocent civilians were needlessly killed.
- The war could have been ended less painfully with a blockade and conventional bombing.
- The use of nuclear weapons cast a shadow over the world that remains to this day.

What do you think?

Question 2: Should peaceful nuclear energy be developed further?

Yes!

- Within 50 years the world's supplies of oil and gas will have run out. We need to start building up all possible replacement energy sources now.
- Wind and water power will never meet all the world's energy needs.
- Modern technology means that accidents like Chernobyl are now virtually impossible.
- By developing nuclear energy we prevent oil- and gas-producing states from holding too much power in the world.
- Possible pollution from radioactive nuclear waste is much less of a threat than the greenhouse gases produced by burning oil and gas.

No!

- Even sealed in concrete drums, nuclear waste may remain dangerous for 10,000 years. We should not leave such a terrible legacy for future generations.
- Nuclear power plants can never be 100 percent safe. The more there are, the greater the chances of another Chernobyl-style catastrophe.
- The spread of nuclear technology would increase the chances of the spread of nuclear weapons.
- Power produced by nuclear energy is very expensive.
- Green energy production is in its early stages. In time it will easily meet all our needs.

What do you think?

| Anti-nuclear campaigners protest against the transportation of nuclear waste in Germany, 2004. |

Find Out More

Using the Internet

Explore the Internet to find out more about Hiroshima and nuclear power. You can use a search engine, such as www.yahooligans.com or www.google.com, and type in keywords or phrases such as *atom bomb*, *Manhattan Project*, *Truman*, *radioactivity*, or *Chernobyl*.

More Books to Read

Dowswell, Paul. *The Causes of World War II.*
   Chicago: Heinemann Library, 2003.

Harris, Nathaniel. *Witness to History: Hiroshima.*
   Chicago: Heinemann Library, 2004.

Saunders, Nigel, and Steven Chapman. *Energy Essentials: Nuclear Energy.*
   Chicago: Raintree, 2005.

Tames, Richard. *Pearl Harbor: The U.S. Enters World War II.*
   Chicago: Heinemann Library, 2006.

Timeline

1639	Japan cuts off foreign trade
1853	The United States forces Japan to re-open foreign trade
1894	Japan defeats China and takes over Taiwan
1905	Japan defeats Russia
1910	Japan takes over Korea
1923	Earthquake destroys Tokyo and Yokohama
1924	The United States bans immigration by Japanese
1929	World trade collapses
1931	Japan takes over Manchuria
1937	Japan attempts to conquer all of China
1941	**December 7** Japan attacks U.S. naval base at Pearl Harbor, Hawaii
1942	**June** Japanese navy defeated by the United States at the Battle of Midway
1944	The United States begins bombing of Japan
1945	**March** U.S. bombers devastate Tokyo
	April U.S. forces invade Okinawa
	May Germany surrenders
	July 16 First successful atom bomb test at Alamagordo air base, New Mexico
	August 6 Atom bomb dropped on Hiroshima
	August 8 USSR declares war on Japan
	August 9 Atom bomb dropped on Nagasaki
	August 14 Japan surrenders
	August 28 U.S. troops land in Japan
1949	North Atlantic Treaty Organization founded
1951	Peace treaty signed between Japan and the United States
1952	The United States tests first hydrogen bomb
1954	USS *Nautilus* launched
1955	USSR found the Warsaw Pact
1964	Olympic Games held in Tokyo
1974	India tests an atomic bomb
1979	Nuclear radiation leak at Three Mile Island, Pennsylvania
1986	Nuclear reactor meltdown at Chernobyl, Ukraine
1991	Breakup of USSR ends the Cold War

Glossary

allies	friendly nations
blockade	use ships to prevent goods from entering a country
boon	something that is useful
cataract	clouding of the lens of the eye, causing loss of sight
cobalt	silver-white metal that can be made radioactive to cure some kinds of cancer
colony	land in one place ruled by a foreign government in another place
communism	system of government based on the idea that a single ruling political party can run a country for all its people's benefit better than if they are left to make their own decisions and keep their own private homes, land, and businesses
democracy	system of government based on the idea that all citizens have equal rights to speak on political matters and take part freely in choosing and changing their leaders
disarmament	giving up weapons
extremist	someone with such strong views that he or she is not prepared to compromise
fanatic	extremist who is prepared to use violence
guerrilla	irregular fighter, not part of a recognized army
immigration	when people move from one country to live in another country
intimidate	frighten
kilowatts	1,000 watts; a watt is the basic unit for measuring electricity
negotiation	settle a problem or dispute by talking; usually both sides agree to give up part of their demands
occupation	rule by a foreign army
radiation	energy given off by atomic material
refugee	person forced to leave his or her home or country
sabotage	deliberate damage to stop something from working properly
Soviet	belonging to the Soviet Union (USSR)
trade union	organization to protect and improve the rights and interests of workers
treaty	official agreement between different countries
USSR	Union of Soviet Socialist Republics; an empire in which communist Russia controlled neighboring countries from 1917 to 1991

Index